ANIMALS ON THE BRINK
Bald Eagles

Karen Dudley

www.av2books.com

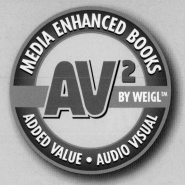

AV² provides enriched content that supplements and complements this book. Weigl's AV² books strive to create inspired learning and engage young minds in a total learning experience.

Your AV² Media Enhanced books come alive with...

Audio
Listen to sections of the book read aloud.

Key Words
Study vocabulary, and complete a matching word activity.

Video
Watch informative video clips.

Quizzes
Test your knowledge.

Go to **www.av2books.com,** and enter this book's unique code.

Embedded Weblinks
Gain additional information for research.

Slide Show
View images and captions, and prepare a presentation.

BOOK CODE

E 7 2 1 0 4

AV² by Weigl brings you media enhanced books that support active learning.

Try This!
Complete activities and hands-on experiments.

... and much, much more!

Published by AV² by Weigl
350 5th Avenue, 59th Floor
New York, NY 10118
Websites: www.av2books.com   www.weigl.com

Library of Congress Control Number: 2013953036

ISBN 978-1-4896-0552-8 (hardcover)
ISBN 978-1-4896-0553-5 (softcover)
ISBN 978-1-4896-0554-2 (single-user eBook)
ISBN 978-1-4896-0555-9 (multi-user eBook)

Printed in the United States of America in North Mankato, Minnesota
1 2 3 4 5 6 7 8 9   17 16 15 14 13

122013
WEP301113

Project Coordinator Aaron Carr
Design Mandy Christiansen

Every reasonable effort has been made to trace ownership and to obtain permission to reprint copyright material. The publishers would be pleased to have any errors or omissions brought to their attention so that they may be corrected in subsequent printings.

Photo Credits
Weigl acknowledges Getty Images as its primary photo supplier for this title.

Contents

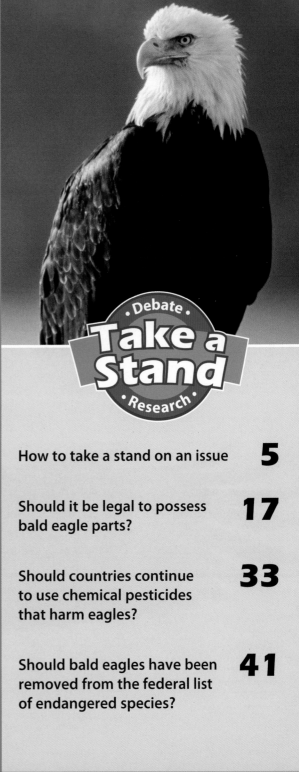

How to take a stand on an issue **5**

Should it be legal to possess bald eagle parts? **17**

Should countries continue to use chemical pesticides that harm eagles? **33**

Should bald eagles have been removed from the federal list of endangered species? **41**

The Bald Eagle

Bald eagles are among the largest and most powerful birds in the world. They are sometimes called the lions of the sky. In North America, these birds are second in size only to the California condor. Eagles are a symbol of strength in many different cultures, yet there is much more to the bird than power.

In this book, you will learn about the four different groups of eagles. You will find out where the expression "eagle-eyed" comes from. You will learn what bald eagles eat and how they hunt. You will also find out why you should never disturb a bald eagle when it is sitting in its nest.

Some populations of bald eagles began declining in the 1800s. Although these populations have recovered, their troubles have not been forgotten. Problems caused by humans continue to affect the ability of the bald eagle to thrive. These problems include destruction of **habitats**, hunting, use of **pesticides**, and other pollutants. Read on, and find out why bald eagles were at risk, what is happening today, and how to support the bald eagle.

Only a mature eagle has a completely white head and tail.

The bald eagle is the only eagle found solely in North America.

How to Take a Stand on an Issue

Research is important to the study of any scientific field. When scientists choose a subject to study, they must conduct research to ensure they have a thorough understanding of the topic. They ask questions about the subject and then search for answers. Sometimes, however, there is no clear answer to a question. In these cases, scientists must use the information they have to form a hypothesis, or theory. They must take a stand on one side of an issue or the other. Follow the process below for each Take a Stand section in this book to determine where you stand on these issues.

1. **What is the Issue?**
   a. Determine a research subject, and form a general question about the subject.

2. **Form a Hypothesis**
   a. Search at the library and online for sources of information on the subject.
   b. Conduct basic research on the subject to narrow down the general question.
   c. Form a hypothesis on the subject based on research to this point.
   d. Make predictions based on the hypothesis. What are the expected results?

3. **Research the Issue**
   a. Conduct extensive research using a variety of sources, including books, scientific journals, and reliable websites.
   b. Collect data on the issue and take notes on all information gathered from research.
   c. Draw conclusions based on the information collected.

4. **Conclusion**
   a. Explain the research findings.
   b. Was the hypothesis proved or disproved?

Eagle
Extras

A young bald eagle can be difficult to identify. It has no white head or tail feathers, just speckled brown feathers all over.

A bald eagle's skeleton weighs less than half of what its feathers weigh.

Features

Eagles are divided into four groups. They are the snake eagles, buzzard-like eagles, booted eagles, and sea and fish eagles. The bald eagle belongs to the last group. The golden eagle, the other North American eagle, is a booted eagle.

Sea and fish eagles prey mostly on **aquatic** animals. They have long talons, or claws, and spiky knobs on their toes. These features help them to hold on to slippery prey.

Bald eagles are not really bald. Instead, their heads are covered with white feathers. The bald eagle's scientific name, *Haliaeetus leucocephalus*, actually means "white-headed sea eagle." People call the eagle "bald" after the word *piebald*, which describes markings that are two colors, usually black and white.

The size of a bald eagle can vary, depending on its age, its gender, and where it lives. Immature eagles are often larger than adults. This is because a young eagle's tail and wing feathers are longer. Despite these longer feathers, immature eagles weigh less than adults.

The female bald eagle is typically larger than the male. There are many possible reasons for this. Some biologists believe that the larger size helps females defend their nest, eggs, and young. The smaller males can maneuver more easily, so they are better able to defend their territory. The female bald eagle has a wingspan of more than 7 feet (2 meters). The male has a wingspan of only 6 feet (1.8 m).

Bald eagles in captivity have lived for almost 50 years. Wild eagles probably have a much shorter life span. Disease and starvation are bigger risks for them. In addition, eagles often die when they come into contact with humans or human settlements. Wild eagles may be electrocuted by power lines, hit by vehicles, shot by hunters, or poisoned by pesticides.

Classification

Eagles are birds of prey. This means that they eat other animals to survive. Birds of prey are also called raptors. There are two main **orders** of raptors. They are the Strigiformes and the Falconiformes. The Strigiformes order includes all owls. These birds hunt mostly at night. The Falconiformes order includes eagles, vultures, hawks, falcons, ospreys, and secretary birds. They hunt mostly during the day. There are more than 60 eagle **species** in the world. Of these, there are eight species of sea eagles.

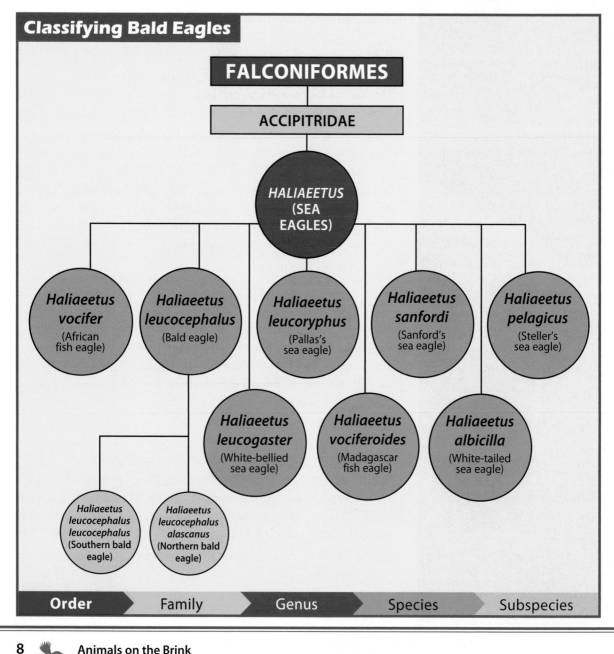

Classifying Bald Eagles

FALCONIFORMES

ACCIPITRIDAE

HALIAEETUS (SEA EAGLES)

Haliaeetus vocifer (African fish eagle)

Haliaeetus leucocephalus (Bald eagle)

Haliaeetus leucoryphus (Pallas's sea eagle)

Haliaeetus sanfordi (Sanford's sea eagle)

Haliaeetus pelagicus (Steller's sea eagle)

Haliaeetus leucogaster (White-bellied sea eagle)

Haliaeetus vociferoides (Madagascar fish eagle)

Haliaeetus albicilla (White-tailed sea eagle)

Haliaeetus leucocephalus leucocephalus (Southern bald eagle)

Haliaeetus leucocephalus alascanus (Northern bald eagle)

Order → Family → Genus → Species → Subspecies

Of all the sea eagles, the bald eagle and the African fish eagle look most alike. Both species have white head and tail feathers, but the bald eagle has a yellow beak and no white feathers on its chest.

The African fish eagle lives in Africa south of the Sahara Desert.

The white-tailed sea eagle is the largest bird of prey in Great Britain.

Special Adaptations

Bald eagles have certain features that they share with other flying birds. These adaptations make it possible for the birds to fly and survive.

Skeleton

The skeleton of the bald eagle is made of thin, hollow bones. The light skeleton makes it easier for the eagle to fly. Many of the eagle's bones are fused, or joined, which makes them very strong. This kind of skeleton helps to support the birds as they fly.

Feathers

A bald eagle feather is made up of a central shaft with many branches, or barbs. Each barb has hundreds of tiny hooks that stick to one another. The feather is strong as long as the barbs stay locked together by the hooks. Feathers help support the eagle when it flies. The layered feathers also shed rainwater to help keep the eagle's body dry.

Talons

Bald eagles have three toes in front and one behind. On the tips of their toes, they have long, curved talons. These razor-sharp talons are an eagle's most important weapon. When a bald eagle grasps its prey, the hind talons dig deep into the victim.

Beak

Like other birds, bald eagles have no teeth. They must swallow their food in pieces. Using their huge hooked beaks, they tear up prey into bite-sized morsels. Sometimes, if the eagle's talons have not already ended the prey's life, a sharp jab of the bird's beak is needed.

Eyes

The resolution, or clarity, of a bald eagle's vision is exceptional. This sharp vision is partly due to the eagle's large eyes. A flexible neck also allows the eagle to turn its head three quarters of a circle around to see in different directions. The bald eagle's inner eyelids, called nictating membranes, help keep the eyes moist and protected from dust, wind, and Sun.

Feet

Bald eagles have very strong feet that they use for capturing prey. The undersides of the feet are rough, like sandpaper. This helps the eagle hold on to slippery fish or snakes. Compared to their body size, bald eagles have large feet, up to 6 inches (15 centimeters) long.

Eagle
Extras

White splotches of solid waste at the foot of a tree or cliff indicate an eagle roosting site. This "whitewash" builds up over time.

A group of eagles is sometimes called a convocation.

Groups

How much bald eagles socialize depends on the time of year. Adult eagles are busy with nesting activities in the spring and summer. During this time, breeding pairs stay close to their own territory. They rarely interact with other bald eagles, except to chase off intruders. Eagles that are too young to mate spend the warmer months exploring, learning about their environment, and trying to survive.

In the winter, and during **migration**, bald eagles are more sociable. Large groups of eagles often gather together around an abundant food source. Biologists believe these winter gatherings may provide a place for young adult eagles to meet mates.

In the winter, bald eagles are less active than they are during the summer nesting season. A low activity level helps them conserve energy during the colder weather. More than 90 percent of their day is spent sleeping or dozing in the Sun. In the remaining time, they look for food and eat.

Bald eagles find food in two ways. They forage, or fly around in search of food. They also watch to see where other eagles are gathering. When many eagles gather in or circle around one area, other eagles know that food is available there. A bald eagle can see a circling group from as far away as 40 miles (65 kilometers). In this way, a bald eagle may be able to get a meal without using a great deal of energy trying to find it. Stealing another eagle's food is common.

The best example of bald eagles feeding in groups occurs on the Chilkat River, in Alaska. In the autumn and early winter, salmon spawn, or lay their eggs, and then die in this river. Many eagles gather to feast on the remains of the fish. More than 3,000 bald eagles have been seen in a 36-mile (60-km) stretch of the river.

During the winter, groups of eagles spend the night close together on **roosts**. Two birds may roost together in a tree, or more than 500 may roost in a small group of trees. Often the same roosting sites are used year after year.

In the morning, the eagles often leave the roosting site, one after another. They gather again at a feeding site. Following older, more experienced eagles helps young, inexperienced eagles learn where to find food.

Eagle Extras

An eagle will try to protect its territory or prey with a high-pitched threat call.

Perching areas can be noisy as the bald eagles defend their space.

Communication

Bald eagles communicate with one another in a variety of ways. They make and respond to a number of different calls. In addition, visual displays play an important role in bald eagle communication.

Bald eagle sounds range from a harsh cry to a low, snickering call. Eagles make noises to greet a mate or warn off intruders. Young eagles make a peeping or whining call to beg for food from their parents. When eagles gather in the winter, they are often quite vocal, especially when they have hunted successfully or stolen another eagle's dinner.

One example of bald eagle communication takes place at the roosting site. If one eagle lands too close to another, the perched eagle will hiss and threaten the newcomer. If the new eagle is larger or older than the other, it may push out a smaller, younger bird. The smaller, younger eagle is then forced to find another spot and may try to push another eagle from its perch. This whole process of communication can begin again with each new arrival. It continues until each eagle is comfortable or until night falls.

"For a season, I was privileged to live with a pair of bald eagles . . . watching as they courted, built a home, and raised a family with a tenderness and caring entirely at odds with my preconceived notions."
Scott Nielsen

Scott Nielsen is a bird biologist and photographer. His photographs have appeared in many North American nature publications, calendars, posters, and books. He is the author of *A Season with Eagles*, which he wrote after spending a season watching and photographing an eagle pair raise its family.

Body Language

It is common for animals to use body language to give information to other members of their species. Body language is an essential part of how bald eagles communicate. Bald eagles use their feathers, wings, and bodies to communicate with one another.

Mock Attacking

An eagle defending its territory will chase or circle over an intruder until it leaves the area. If one eagle spots another eagle that is feeding, it may raise its wings and talons and try to appear larger. The bald eagle is engaging in a mock attack to try to chase the other bird from its food.

Roller-Coaster Flight Display

Courtship displays take place each breeding season, even between birds that have been mated for a long time. One of the ways that birds court is flight displays. One eagle may perform a roller-coaster display, flying up and down in a continuous motion like a roller coaster.

Perching

Bald eagles perch in trees or on cliffs where other birds can easily see them. This helps them defend their territory without fighting, as their distinctive plumage warns other birds to stay away.

Cartwheeling

In the cartwheel display, a courting pair begins by flying up very high. Then, one eagle positions itself upside down beneath the other. The two eagles lock talons and begin to roll, first one on top, then the other. The entire time, they beat their wings to slow their fall. Just before reaching the ground, they separate and begin again. Eagles may tumble for several thousand feet (meters) in this fashion.

Should it be legal to possess bald eagle parts?

It is illegal to kill or capture bald eagles in the United States without a permit. Under the Bald and Golden Eagle Protection Act of 1940, people may use eagle parts for scientific, exhibition, and religious purposes.

FOR

1. The U.S. Fish and Wildlife Service's National Eagle Repository collects and distributes eagle parts to indigenous peoples for religious purposes. This practice harms no birds, as the parts come from eagles found dead by government agencies, zoos, and other groups.
2. Certain organizations may possess bald eagle parts, nests, and eggs. The work of these groups contributes to scientific knowledge and educates the public.

AGAINST

1. Without complete protection, bald eagles are at risk. Unless there is a total ban on owning bald eagle parts, people will be encouraged to hunt for trophies.
2. Profiting from the illegal taking of eagles is always a concern. Exceptions to the law against taking these birds may lead to the hunting of raptor populations.

Eagle
Extras

Bald eagles build the
largest bird nests in
North America.

Bald eagles often build their nests in the tallest
trees available. This helps them watch for danger.

Mating and Birth

The mating season of bald eagles occurs at different times of the year, depending on where the birds live. In Arizona, eagles build nests and lay their eggs in September. In Texas and Florida, bald eagles nest in November or December. By nesting at these times, the eagles make sure their young bald eagles, called eaglets, will not hatch during the hottest part of the year.

Bald eagles that live in more northern areas are troubled by cold rather than heat when nesting. Eagles in northern Canada and Alaska often do not nest until mid-May, after the coldest weather has passed. If eggs are laid too early in these areas, they may freeze.

A bald eagle's ideal nesting site must have a number of features. Those features include a view of the surrounding area, open areas for clear flight paths, close access to water, and a place for the **aerie**. A mated pair often returns to the same nest each season. They make the nest larger and stronger every year.

Bald eagles in California may nest on top of giant cacti. Eagles in the treeless Aleutian Islands of Alaska nest on the ground. Eagles that live in forested areas prefer to build their aeries in large, sturdy trees. Bald eagles rarely build a nest at the very top of a tree, because the branches are not strong enough to hold the nest's weight. An old, well-established aerie may weigh up to 2 tons (1.8 tonnes). Eagles usually build a nest about 80 feet (24 m) above the ground on a forked branch about 20 feet (6 m) from the top of the tree.

Both male and female eagles help build the nest. They use sticks, dead branches, grasses, cattails, mosses, and other plant material. A new nest takes about one week to complete. If the eagles are fixing up an old nest, it takes them only a few days to finish.

A typical nest is as much as 6 feet (1.8 m) wide and 4 feet (1.2 m) tall. However, if an aerie is used over many years, it can be much larger. One nest in Florida was almost 10 feet (3 m) wide and 20 feet (6 m) tall.

Once the aerie is finished and the eagles have mated, the female becomes sluggish as eggs form inside her. This period of inactivity, which includes the time when the eggs are laid, usually lasts for about one week. During this period, the male eagle brings food to his mate.

Eaglets

Bald eagles may lay one to four eggs, but two is the most common number. Northern bald eagles often lay more eggs than do southern eagles. Bald eagle eggs are dull white and can weigh 4.5 ounces (130 grams). They measure 3.5 inches (9 cm) by 2.5 inches (6 cm). The eggs are laid two to four days apart.

Until all the eggs are laid, the female eagle stays in the nest. When she is finished laying her eggs, both parents take turns sitting on the eggs to keep them warm. This warmth **incubates** the eggs. Incubating eagles sit very low in the nest, using their bodies as shields to protect the eggs from **predators** and from extreme weather conditions.

The eggs are incubated for about 35 days. They usually hatch a few days apart because they are not laid at the same time. When the eggs are almost ready to hatch, the adult eagles start to sit higher in the nest. Biologists think the eagles do this because they can sense movement within the eggs and do not want to crush an emerging eaglet.

Newly hatched eaglets depend completely on their parents for food and protection. Although eaglets are born with a coat of soft, fluffy feathers called down, they cannot keep themselves warm. A parent must crouch down in the nest, keeping the young birds warm beneath its body and protecting them from rain, snow, and wind. This protective behavior is known as brooding. Parent eagles must brood their young for at least one month. After this time, the eaglets will have grown a second coat of down and be able to keep themselves warm.

Feeding hungry eaglets is almost a full-time job. Parents rip the prey into small pieces that the eaglets can swallow. Feedings take place every three to four hours. After six or seven weeks, the parents' job gets easier, because the eaglets are able to rip prey apart by themselves.

The first egg that hatches usually has the largest, heaviest eaglet.

Eagle
Extras

A nesting bald eagle develops a featherless patch on its underside. This area allows warmth to pass more easily from the bird's body to the eggs.

When young eaglets squeal and peep in a food-begging call, the parents are quick to bring food to the nest.

Eagle
Extras

By the time an eaglet has become an adult bald eagle, it will have more than 7,000 feathers.

As their down is replaced by stronger feathers, juvenile bald eagles look rather ragged and messy.

Development

A newly hatched eaglet does not look anything like its parents. Its eyes are closed, and its head wobbles around on a neck that seems too thin. A young eaglet's bare legs are pink. The rest of it is covered with down. After about four hours, it will open its eyes for the first time. A newly hatched eaglet weighs about 3 ounces (85 grams).

After about three weeks, the soft gray down is replaced by thicker, longer, darker-colored down. The eaglet's legs turn bright yellow, and its beak darkens to a bluish-black. Unlike its yellow-eyed parents, a young eaglet has dark brown eyes. The eaglet grows rapidly, gaining about 4 ounces (113 g) of weight each day. By three weeks of age, the young bird weighs about 5 pounds (2.3 kg) and measures 1 foot (30 cm) high.

Over the next few weeks, the eaglet's immature plumage starts to grow in, and the young eagle continues to grow quickly. Eaglets often squabble with one another over food. They also shuffle around the nest, building up strength in their legs. They **preen** often, learning how to take care of their feathers.

Bald eagles **fledge** 8 to 14 weeks after hatching. Most begin flying at about 10 weeks. By this time, the young birds weigh about 11 pounds (5 kg). This is almost their full adult weight.

As the eaglets' juvenile feathers grow in, the young birds become more active around the nest. They practice their hunting skills by jumping on imaginary prey. They play by taking sticks away from each other or by throwing twigs in the air and catching them in their talons. They also strengthen their flight muscles by flapping their wings. Sometimes, during all this activity, an unfledged eaglet may tumble from the nest. Eaglets often spend their last few flightless days on the ground or perched on a low branch. When this happens, the parents bring food to their youngster until it fledges.

Male eaglets usually fledge a few days earlier than females. For the first few weeks after fledging, young eagles practice their new skills close to the nest site. They still rely on their parents for food, but they also begin to forage. About 6 to 10 weeks after fledging, they begin to make their own way in the world.

Bald eagles go through four **molts** of immature plumage before growing adult plumage. The eagles get their adult plumage when they are between four and five years of age. At this time, they are ready to mate.

Habitat

Bald eagles like to live near water. They live along seacoasts, beside lakes and rivers, or even in swamplands. Wherever eagles live, they are never far from a river or shoreline. Bald eagle habitats usually include two specific kinds of areas. One is a foraging area, in which food is always available and plentiful. This area must also include open spaces, such as beaches and sandbars, where prey can be captured and eaten.

A proper perching area is also important. When an eagle perches in an exposed area, it is letting others know the territory is occupied. A perching area may include tall trees, rocks, cliffs, logs, ice, or even fence posts and poles. These are places where eagles can rest, stand guard, or watch for prey.

Organizing the Seacoast

Earth is home to millions of different **organisms**, all of which have specific survival needs. These organisms rely on their environment, or the place where they live, for their survival. All plants and animals have relationships with their environment. They interact with the environment itself, as well as the other plants and animals within the environment. These interactions create **ecosystems**.

Ecosystems can be broken down into levels of organization. These levels range from a single plant or animal to many species of plants and animals living together in an area.

Organism
A single organism

Population
Many organisms of the same species

Community
Several species living together

Biosphere
Planet Earth and all of its living things

Ecosystem
Many species of plants and animals in an area

Wherever they live, eagle pairs work together to keep a lookout for prey.

Eagle Extras

Eagles sometimes use trash for their nests. Scientists have found plastic bottles, clothespins, lightbulbs, and golf balls built into bald eagle nests.

Like other soaring birds, bald eagles have specially adapted primary feathers. When held a certain way, these primaries form gaps that allow the eagles to better control their flight.

Range

Bald eagles have three levels of territories. They are the nest site, the breeding territory, and the home range. A home range is the area in which bald eagles search for food. Its size depends on the amount of food that is available and on the number of other bald eagles in the area. In general, home ranges are a minimum of 4 to 6 square miles (10 to 15 square kilometers). Ranges are larger in places where food is scarce. Bald eagles do not defend their home ranges.

Breeding territories are a different matter. Bald eagles will defend this territory against any intruders. A breeding territory is about 0.4 to 0.8 square miles (1 to 2 sq. km) in size. Often, it is long and narrow. To fishing birds such as the bald eagle, water is more important than land. As a result, a breeding territory often stretches along the length of a river or shoreline. The nest site is located within a bald eagle's breeding territory.

From an Expert

"Some condemn [the bald eagle] for its destructive powers; others consider it an unworthy symbol of the United States because of its . . . lifestyle; many regard it with special pride because it symbolizes freedom and independence. Still others, especially those fortunate enough to have seen a wild eagle, appreciate it as an important component of a natural ecosystem."
Mark Stalmaster

Mark Stalmaster was a park ranger before becoming a wildlife biologist. He has worked with bald eagles for many years, observing them and raising them in captivity. Stalmaster is the author of *The Bald Eagle*.

Migration

Migration is regular seasonal movement from a winter range to a summer range and back again. Most eagle populations migrate north in late winter or early spring. In the fall, they migrate south. Some bald eagles in warmer southern areas do not migrate at all. They live in the same region year-round. Others migrate north in midsummer or late summer, then back south in the fall. Migrating bald eagles often fly between the same summer and winter ranges.

Bald eagles often travel later in the day during spring migration than during fall migration. The reason relates to the availability of air currents known as thermals. When sunlight heats Earth's surface, masses of warm air rise in columns called thermals. Bald eagles ride these thermals by stretching their wings and soaring upward. In spring, thermals are at their best during late afternoon in many western U.S. states and Canadian provinces.

Biologists believe that a decline of food supply triggers fall migration. As long as there is enough food, eagles prefer to stay where they are. Cold weather is not a problem for bald eagles. For eagles living in northern areas, problems arise when waterfowl, a favorite prey, begin to migrate south. The situation worsens when rivers and streams freeze over and bald eagles cannot reach the fish. Without fish or waterfowl, the eagles are left with few food sources. As food becomes scarce, bald eagles head south.

Fall migration takes place mainly during October and November. Bald eagles almost always migrate alone. Even mated pairs split up to make the journey. The eagles usually begin to migrate in the late morning or early afternoon. They often continue until dusk. If the weather becomes snowy or overcast, eagles will often wait until it clears.

Younger eagles are usually the first to head south in the fall and the last to arrive on the winter ground. Unfamiliar with the migration route, they often wander off course. Some may even die of starvation if they are unable to find an adequate wintering spot.

A migrating bald eagle may travel up to 270 miles (435 km) in a single day.

Despite their graceful appearance, bald eagles can be awkward flyers without perfect wind conditions.

Diet

Bald eagles are both hunters and **scavengers**. Their ability to eat many types of food helps them survive in an environment where prey may sometimes be difficult to find. A bald eagle's diet is made up of fish, birds, and **mammals**. Eagles prefer to eat fish. They hunt for types of fish that swim near the surface of the water, because these fish are easy to see and catch.

Waterfowl, such as geese and ducks, are also a favorite prey. Bald eagles will hunt just about any kind of waterbird or seabird, especially injured or sick ones. Eagles eat mammals when fish or birds cannot be found. Eagles capture and eat smaller mammals, such as mice, muskrats, and squirrels. They also scavenge the meat off larger mammals, such as deer or seals, that have died. These dead animals are called carrion.

Like vultures, bald eagles are always on the lookout for a meal of carrion.

Bald eagles usually eat about 6 to 11 percent of their body weight each day, though healthy eagles can go for a week without food. They need more food in winter because they use more energy to keep warm. An eagle's stomach is small. When it finds or captures a large amount of food, it stores some of the food in its **crop**. A full-grown eagle can keep about 32 ounces (900 g) of food in its crop. This allows the eagle to store food for times when prey is scarce.

Bald eagles have several hunting and foraging techniques. They prefer to eat whatever is available with the least amount of effort. Bald eagles steal fish from osprey in midair and chase vultures away from carrion. Eagles will even swoop down on a sea otter, snatching the otter's meal off its belly.

Bald eagles hunt when they cannot steal or scavenge. Eagles catch their food with their talons. Sometimes, a fish may be too large for an eagle to lift in the air. When this happens, the eagle flaps its wings and swims awkwardly to shore, towing its catch in its talons.

Eagles can see up to three times more clearly than humans. This is why sharp-sighted people are often called "eagle-eyed."

Once the eagle spots its prey, it drops down quickly with its talons extended. This is called stooping.

The Food Cycle

A food cycle shows how energy in the form of food is passed from one living thing to another. For example, microscopic animals are food for fish, which are food for a bald eagle. Every animal survives by eating plants or animals in its food cycle. Bald eagles belong to many food cycles. In the diagram below, the arrows show the flow of energy from one living thing to the next through a **food web**.

Producers
Tiny plants called **plankton** that live in the ocean use sunlight to produce food energy. Grasses, trees, herbs, and shrubs also produce food energy using sunlight.

Primary Consumers
Many sea animals eat plankton in the water. Deer, geese, ducks, and rodents get food energy from eating grasses, trees, herbs, and shrubs.

Secondary Consumers
Larger fish, as well as sea mammals such as seals and sea lions, hunt the smaller fish that live on plankton.

Tertiary Consumers

Bald eagles feed on a variety of secondary consumers, such as fish and seal carrion. They also eat deer carrion and catch primary consumers, including waterfowl, mice, muskrats, and squirrels.

Parasites

Bald eagles provide a home for parasites such as the wormlike creatures called helminths.

Decomposers

When an eagle dies, decomposers break down the eagle's body materials. This adds nutrients to the soil.

Take a Stand

·Debate·
·Research·

Should countries continue to use chemical pesticides that harm eagles?

Agricultural pests, which damage or destroy crops, include insects, bacteria, fungi, viruses, birds, and rodents. Chemical pesticides kill pests and increase the amounts of crops that farmers can harvest and sell.

FOR

1. Feeding the world's growing population is a high priority. Losing crops that humans eat or that are used to feed livestock is too high a price to pay to protect some eagles.
2. Not all chemicals are harmful, and harmful ones can be used carefully. Pesticides can reduce pest populations. Then, farmers can trap or sterilize insects to limit the growth of the population.

AGAINST

1. Modern agriculture offers better options for controlling insects and pests. By changing crops each year or controlling soil nutrients, farmers can control pests without using any chemicals.
2. Bald eagle and other animal populations are not the only groups affected by chemical pesticides. Many of these pesticides are also harmful to humans. No matter how carefully a pesticide is used, it still ends up in the environment, where it can harm both people and wildlife.

Since they are such heavy birds, bald eagles require tall, strong trees. Loggers have cut down some of these nesting, roosting, and perching sites for bald eagles.

Competition

Adult bald eagles are so large and powerful that they usually win any competition with other birds. Other predators and scavengers also look for food at salmon spawning pools, but bald eagles win a large portion of the dead fish.

By far, a bald eagle's worst enemies are humans. As human populations have grown and settled areas have spread, bald eagles have lost much of their traditional habitat. Land that has not been converted to farms and cities has often been damaged by pesticides and other pollutants.

Bald eaglets compete with each other while they are still in the nest. Eaglets compete aggressively for food with their siblings. Although one researcher has observed bald eagle parents preventing their eaglets from fighting, this discipline is not common.

Adult bald eagles often compete with one another for food. A larger, heavier eagle is quick to snatch a meal away from a smaller eagle. Sometimes, the two will scuffle, each trying to hold on to a piece of the prey. The two eagles may even lock talons. Aggressive bald eagles are more likely to chase off potential thieves.

Adult eagles may also compete with one another for nesting territory. Once a pair has established its territory, the eagles advertise their presence by perching and by calling out to warn off other birds. Often, other eagles avoid the established pair, so conflicts are rare. If another adult eagle does venture into an established territory, the mated pair will chase it off. Immature intruders are also chased away, but often not as aggressively.

Bald eagles rely on their powerful feet and sharp talons for more than hunting. When defending itself, a bald eagle will sometimes lean back and rake enemies with its talons.

Bald Eagles with Other Animals

Bald eagles compete with other birds and animals for food, and sometimes other birds or animals prey on eagles. Eagle eggs and newly hatched eaglets are helpless against seagulls, owls, gray squirrels, red squirrels, raccoons, and crows. Bald eagle parents must be on guard against these predators at all times.

Other animals will also try to steal food from bald eagles. A coyote may succeed in chasing an eagle away from a carcass. Sometimes, crows and seagulls steal small parts of a bald eagle's dinner. Most of the time, however, the eagle will fight off the other animal.

Eagles compete with humans for both food and territory. Most of the time, eagles lose the competition. Eagles need old forests with tall trees in which to build their nests. When European settlers first moved to North America, many of these forests were cut down to make way for farms and cities. When this happened, eagles had little choice but to leave the area and try to find other nest sites.

Eagles rely mainly on fish for their diet, but people also use this resource. As humans reduce fish stocks, eagles have a harder time finding enough food. Another problem in eagle-human relationships has to do with waterfowl. Both eagles and humans hunt these waterbirds for food.

Human hunters sometimes use lead shot in their guns. Lead shot is poisonous when it is dissolved. Sometimes, eagles eat birds that have been injured by lead shot. The lead shot then dissolves in the eagle's stomach, slowly poisoning the bird. Although using lead shot was banned in 1991 for waterfowl, hunters in the United States continue to fire about 3,000 tons (2,700 tonnes) of lead into the environment every year.

The bald eagle's excellent vision allows it to see hidden prey. When a human might see only a hump of beige fur, a bald eagle will see five distinctly colored ground squirrels.

Eagle parents must be on guard against any threats to the eaglets. Owls or other eagles will prey on a helpless eaglet if they get a chance.

Folklore

Eagles are found in the folklore and legends of many cultures. Some myths about eagles relate to their abilities. Since eagles are able to soar high in the sky, people associated eagles with the Sun. The Sun was also often linked to royalty. An eagle's presence was therefore believed to predict the birth of kings or other important royal events.

In many cultures, eagles were thought to be messengers of the gods because they were so powerful and could fly so high. Ancient Greeks believed the gods would not harm their own messengers with lightning. Eagles were tied to the roofs of Greek temples to prevent lightning from striking. Ancient Romans and Greeks also believed that eagles had healing power. Eagle talons, feathers, and bones were often used to make medicines. In Babylon, the souls of rulers were believed to rise to heaven on an eagle. Whenever a ruler died, an eagle was released at the funeral so that the ruler's soul could rise to live with the gods.

Eagles often symbolize strength, pride, and power. As a result, the eagle has been a popular symbol with the military in many different times and places. Ancient warriors used eagle feathers for making arrows. They believed these arrows had the strength and speed of the eagle. Each Roman Legion carried a special pole topped with a golden eagle. The Muslim ruler and warrior Saladin had an eagle on his coat of arms. A special group of Aztec warriors was named Eagles. Iroquois warriors wore eagle feathers to symbolize their bravery.

Eagles are also national emblems in many countries. In the United States, the bald eagle stands for power, independence, and victory. In Mexico, the national emblem is an eagle devouring a snake. Symbols including an eagle and a snake also appear in cultures from India, South and Central America, and New Zealand.

Since 1782, the U.S. government has used the great seal of the United States, which includes a bald eagle.

Myth	VS	Fact
Many American colonists believed that eagles preyed on livestock, such as cattle. Today, people sometimes worry about bald eagles swooping down to snatch a family pet.		Although eagles preyed on the grouse, rabbits, and fish that the new settlers hunted, they do not hunt livestock or animals that weigh more than about 5 pounds (2 kg).
Bald eagles are unclean birds that carry disease.		Bald eagles spend a great deal of time keeping their feathers clean. Sometimes, they wade into shallow water to wet their soiled feathers and then perch nearby to dry off and preen. Bald eagles carry no diseases harmful to humans.
Bald eagles look fierce because they are.		A bald eagle's bony eyebrow ridge gives it a fierce appearance. The purpose of this ridge is to help protect the eyes from sunlight, dust, and wind. The ridge also helps protect the eagle's eyes from snapping twigs and struggling prey.

Native totem poles in British Columbia feature an eagle on the top. Eagles are considered rulers of the sky.

People first noticed a drop in bald eagle populations in the late 1800s. Over the next few decades, concern about the decline grew, especially because humans were mostly responsible for it. In 1921, an article in *Ecology* magazine discussed the risk of bald eagles becoming **extinct** in the United States, except for Alaska.

Under the Bald and Golden Eagle Protection Act, passed in 1940, it became illegal, in most cases, to kill a bald eagle or to possess bald eagle feathers, talons, nests, or eggs. It is also against the law to disturb the eagles in any way. In 1952, the act was extended to include Alaska. From the 1950s to the mid-1960s, enforcement of the act was uneven. For example, about 20,000 bald and golden eagles were shot in Texas alone.

A major cause for the decline in the bald eagle population in the mid-20th century was the use of a pesticide called DDT. It was discovered in 1939 that DDT could eliminate insect pests, and the chemical was in frequent use by the late 1940s. In 1951, 106 million pounds (48 million kg) of DDT were used in the United States alone. DDT affected eagle populations by blocking the production of calcium in adult eagles. Calcium is what makes eagle eggshells thick and eagle bones strong.

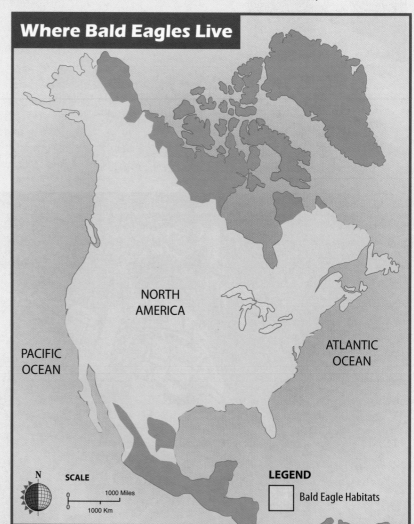

Where Bald Eagles Live

NORTH AMERICA

PACIFIC OCEAN

ATLANTIC OCEAN

N

SCALE

0   1000 Miles

0   1000 Km

LEGEND

Bald Eagle Habitats

As a result of DDT poisoning, many bald eagles laid eggs with shells that were so thin the eggs broke as the parent eagles incubated them. Other eaglets did not get enough calcium for strong bones. Sometimes, eggs rotted without hatching at all. By 1970, only about 1,000 bald eagles were breeding successfully in the United States, not including Alaska.

In the late 1960s, people began to realize how DDT and other pesticides were affecting wildlife. Preserves were established to help protect some of the bald eagles' habitat. The use of DDT was restricted in Canada in 1970. In 1972, it was banned in the United States. This ban and the 1973 **Endangered** Species Act, which gave laws about the environment more power in the United States, helped protect the bald eagle.

The fight to protect the bald eagle in all its native areas has become a conservation success story. In 1995, the status of bald eagles changed from endangered to the lower-risk category of threatened. In 2007, bald eagles were removed from the federal list of protected species.

Today, there are bald eagle populations in every state except Hawai'i, where the eagles have never lived. However, habitat destruction, **poaching**, and poor water quality remain concerns for all animal species, including eagles. Continued conservation efforts are required to maintain the healthy growth of eagle populations.

Should bald eagles have been removed from the federal list of endangered species?

The recovery of the bald eagle was so successful that it is no longer on the federal list of endangered species. Not everyone is convinced that this species no longer needs protection. The bald eagle remains on some state lists of threatened species.

FOR

1. Bald eagles are plentiful in Alaska and Canada. As long as bald eagle populations exist the world, living throughout their native ranges is of no great concern.
2. Even though bald eagles are no longer listed as endangered, they continue to receive protection under the Bald and Golden Eagle Protection Act.

AGAINST

1. The protection of animal species in their entire native ranges is an important part of preserving various ecosystems. It is too early to be sure of the recovery of bald eagle populations in every state.
2. When the bald eagle was an endangered species, its nesting grounds were protected. Developers may now take over important bald eagle habitats and force out the wildlife.

Bald eagles have always been plentiful in Canada as well as in Alaska, where their current estimated population is 30,000.

Saving the Bald Eagle

In 1963, about 400 bald eagle pairs were nesting in the United States, excluding Alaska. Today, there are more than 11,000 pairs in the same area. Many bald eagle experts believe that the continued success of bald eagles depends on how much people want to save them and preserve their habitats. To help people better understand and appreciate bald eagles, biologists and other scientists continue to study and monitor eagles and their populations.

HawkWatch International is an organization dedicated to the conservation of raptors and the environment. HawkWatch scientists have trapped, measured, put leg bands on, and released more than 100,000 raptors. This allows them to track the birds' movements and migrations. By keeping track of banded birds, scientists can also tell if a population consists of old birds, young birds, or a healthy mixture. Each year, they count the number of migrating eagles, hawks, falcons, and other raptors. All this information helps scientists support various species. Satellite tracking also helped HawkWatch scientists identify electrocution by power line as a threat to the survival of raptors. A bald eagle's wingspan is so large that the bird can touch two wires at the same time and get electrocuted.

The U.S. Fish and Wildlife Service has also started a monitoring program for the bald eagle. It will collect data on occupied nests at five-year intervals for 20 years. If the numbers decline enough, the agency will consider expanded monitoring and additional research. Resuming federal protection under the Endangered Species Act is always a possibility if needed.

From an Expert

Priscilla Tucker is a naturalist and a former executive editor for the American Birding Association.

"For more than two hundred years, the bald eagle has symbolized the powerful freedom that is the United States of America. And for most of those two hundred years, the very people who have enjoyed the freedom of living in the United States have shot and poisoned the eagle, eliminated its winter food sources, and encroached on its nesting habitat."

Priscilla Tucker

Back from the Brink

By learning more about bald eagles, you can make better decisions about how to help them. For example, did you know that bald eagles may desert their nest if they are disturbed, especially by humans hiking or camping? Even if there are eggs in the nest, the parents may leave. Their instinct to flee from danger is stronger than their instinct to stay to guard the nest. As the parents feed and care for their young eaglets, usually during the first two weeks, bonding takes place, making nest desertion unlikely. When you are in wilderness areas, try to observe bald eagles and their young from a distance.

There are many other ways to support the growth of raptor populations. One way is to join conservation groups that work to preserve raptor habitats. Find out more about raptor rehabilitation centers near you. Bald eagles and other raptors may be injured in various ways, including colliding with power lines or fences. Many centers in North America accept and nurse these injured birds back to health. They may also offer educational programs or school visits. You can sometimes volunteer to help care for birds at a center.

HawkWatch runs an Adopt-A-Hawk program. In this program, you can "adopt" a banded raptor living in nature. Birds available for adoption include sharp-shinned hawks, American kestrels, golden eagles, and peregrine falcons. You will receive a certificate, a color photo of the bird, and an information sheet about its weight, height, and gender. For more information about bird rehabilitation centers and the Adopt-A-Hawk program, write to:

The Center for Birds of Prey
4872 Seewee Road
Awendaw, SC 29429

HawkWatch International
2240 South 900 East
Salt Lake City, UT 84106

Many birds are mistaken for the immature bald eagle, including golden eagles and turkey vultures.

Activity

Debating helps people think about ideas thoughtfully and carefully. When people debate, two sides take a different viewpoint on a subject. Each side takes turns presenting arguments to support its view.

Use the Take a Stand sections found throughout this book as a starting point for debate topics. Organize your friends or classmates into two teams. One team will argue in favor of the topic, and the other will argue against. Each team should research the issue thoroughly using reliable sources of information, including books, scientific journals, and trustworthy websites. Take notes of important facts that support your side of the debate. Prepare your argument using these facts to support your opinion.

During the debate, the members of each team are given a set amount of time to make their arguments. The team arguing the For side goes first. They have five minutes to present their case. All members of the team should participate equally. Then, the team arguing the Against side presents its arguments. Each team should take notes of the main points the other team argues.

After both teams have made their arguments, they get three minutes to prepare their rebuttals. Teams review their notes from the previous round. The teams focus on trying to disprove each of the main points made by the other team using solid facts. Each team gets three minutes to make its rebuttal. The team arguing the Against side goes first. Students and teachers watching the debate serve as judges. They should try to judge the debate fairly using a standard score sheet, such as the example below.

Criteria	Rate: 1-10	Sample Comments
1. Were the arguments well organized?	8	logical arguments, easy to follow
2. Did team members participate equally?	9	divided time evenly between members
3. Did team members speak loudly and clearly?	3	some members were difficult to hear
4. Were rebuttals specific to the other team's arguments?	6	rebuttals were specific, more facts needed
5. Was respect shown for the other team?	10	all members showed respect to the other team

1. What is a raptor?

2. How many eagle species are there in the world?

3. Why are the undersides of a bald eagle's feet rough like sandpaper?

4. What is an eagle's nest called?

5. How many eggs does a female eagle most often lay?

8. What do bald eagles eat?

6. At what age do eagles begin to leave the nest?

7. What do scientists believe triggers fall migration?

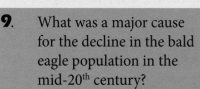

9. What was a major cause for the decline in the bald eagle population in the mid-20th century?

10. How many nesting pairs of bald eagles are there now in the United States, not including Alaska?

Answers:
1. a bird of prey 2. more than 60 3. This helps the eagle hold on to slippery fish or snakes. 4. an aerie 5. two 6. about 6 to 10 weeks old 7. a decline of food supply 8. fish, birds, carrion, and sometimes mice, muskrats, and squirrels 9. the use of a pesticide called DDT that blocked the production of calcium in adult eagles 10. more than 11,000

Key Words

aerie: an eagle's nest

aquatic: living or growing in or on the water

crop: an eagle's pouch between its mouth and stomach, used to store food

ecosystems: communities of living things and resources

endangered: a type of plant or animal that exists in such small numbers that it is in danger of no longer surviving in the world or in a certain area

extinct: no longer surviving in the world or in a certain area

fledge: to learn how to fly; it also means to acquire flight feathers

food web: connecting food chains that show how energy flows from one organism to another through diet

habitats: places where animals live, grow, and raise their young

incubate: to sit on eggs in order to hatch them by the warmth of the body

mammals: warm-blooded animals that have hair or fur and nurse

migration: a regular, seasonal movement to a different region

molts: the shedding feathers that are replaced by a new growth

orders: one of eight major ranks used to classify animals, between class and family

organisms: forms of life

pesticides: chemicals used to kill plant or animal pests

plankton: floating and drifting tiny organisms in the sea

poaching: killing an animal illegally

predators: animals that live by killing other animals for food

preen: to smooth and clean feathers with the beak

roosts: perching trees where eagles spend the night

scavengers: animals that feed on dead animals or plants

species: groups of individuals with common characteristics

Index

Log on to www.av2books.com

AV[2] by Weigl brings you media enhanced books that support active learning. Go to www.av2books.com, and enter the special code found on page 2 of this book. You will gain access to enriched and enhanced content that supplements and complements this book. Content includes video, audio, weblinks, quizzes, a slide show, and activities.

AV[2] Online Navigation

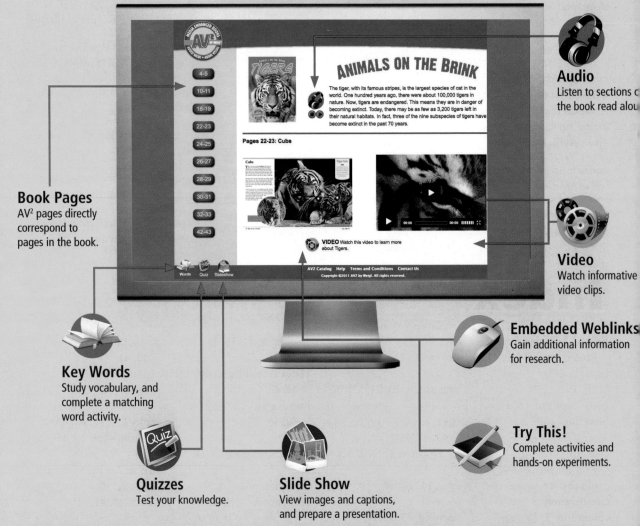

Book Pages
AV[2] pages directly correspond to pages in the book.

Audio
Listen to sections of the book read aloud

Video
Watch informative video clips.

Key Words
Study vocabulary, and complete a matching word activity.

Embedded Weblinks
Gain additional information for research.

Quizzes
Test your knowledge.

Slide Show
View images and captions, and prepare a presentation.

Try This!
Complete activities and hands-on experiments.

AV[2] was built to bridge the gap between print and digital. We encourage you to tell us what you like and what you want to see in the future.

Sign up to be an AV[2] Ambassador at www.av2books.com/ambassador.